THE DREAMS

REINALDO DOMINGOS

dsop editora

AUTHOR
REINALDO DOMINGOS

ILLUSTRATION
TANIA RICCI

INTERNATIONAL EDITORIAL DIRECTOR
ANDRÉ L. PASOTTO

EDITORIAL COORDINATOR
RENATA DE SÁ

ENGLISH VERSION
ANA MILITELLO

ART EDITOR
MAURO ROBERTO FERNANDES

Dados Internacionais de Catalogação na Publicação (CIP)
(Câmara Brasileira do Livro, SP, Brasil)

Domingos, Reinaldo
The dreams / Reinaldo Domingos ; illustration Tania Ricci ; [translation Ana Militello]. -- São Paulo : Editora DSOP, 2020. -- (Explorer)

Título original: O menino e o dinheiro
ISBN 978-65-87565-14-9

1. Dinheiro - Literatura infantojuvenil 2. Finanças - Literatura infantojuvenil I. Ricci, Tania. II. Título. III. Série.

20-43675

Índices para catálogo sistemático:

1. Educação financeira : Literatura infantil 028.5
2. Educação financeira : Literatura infantojuvenil 028.5

Cibele Maria Dias - Bibliotecária - CRB-8/9427

DEAR READER,

MY NAME IS REINALDO, AND JUST LIKE YOU, I WAS ONCE A CHILD. SINCE I WAS LITTLE, I LOVED TO INVENT STORIES AND CREATE IMAGINARY WORLDS. AS I GREW UP, MY BIGGEST DREAM WAS TO SHARE MY STORIES WITH CHILDREN WORLDWIDE.

MY DREAM CAME TRUE. YOU HAVE THE ABILITY TO ACHIEVE YOUR DREAMS TOO. ALL YOU NEED TO DO IS FOLLOW THE FOUR STEPS OF THE METHODOLOGY I CREATED, WHICH YOU WILL LEARN IN THIS BOOK.

BESIDES HELPING YOU TO MAKE YOUR DREAMS COME TRUE, I WANT TO INVITE YOU TO TAKE PART IN THIS STORY WITH ME – BY PAINTING AND DRAWING...

I HOPE YOU ENJOY IT!

ALL THE BEST,

REINALDO DOMINGOS

"EVERY CHILD HAS THE RIGHT TO DREAM,

AND TO MAKE THOSE DREAMS COME TRUE".

Reinaldo Domingos

THERE IS A YOUNG BOY, NICO, WHO LIVES IN A SMALL WHITE HOUSE ON TOP OF THE MOUNTAIN.

FROM THERE, HE CAN SEE THE TOWN FOR MILES AND MILES.

BANK

AT THE FOOT OF THE MOUNTAIN, THERE IS A SMALL RIVER THAT FLOWS DOWNHILL AND FORMS A BIG RIVER.

1 MATCH AND COMPLETE

M __ N __ Y

__ O __ S __

__ O __

T __ E __

PEOPLE FROM WHITE LAKE KNOW WHEN THERE IS A STRANGER IN TOWN. EVEN FROM A DISTANCE, LOOKING UP, THEY CAN SEE EVERYTHING THAT HAPPENS IN THEIR OWN TOWN. THEY KNOW WHO IS COMING, STAYING OR GOING AWAY.

2 LOOK AT THE ITEMS AND **CIRCLE** THE "UP CLOSE" ONE AND MAKE AN **X** ON THE "AT A DISTANCE" ONE.

NICO IS A VERY CURIOUS YOUNG BOY. HE LIKES TO OBSERVE THINGS, NOT ONLY FROM UP CLOSE, BUT FROM A DISTANCE TOO.

3 DRAW A TOY.

... UP CLOSE IN THE CLASSROOM.

... AT A DISTANCE IN THE CLASSROOM.

NICO WATCHES THE ANTS CARRYING SMALL LEAVES INSIDE THE ANTHILL.

4 WRITE AND COLOR.

ANTHILL – ANT

AND THE BIRD COLLECTING SMALL TWIGS TO BUILD A NEST.

5 WRITE AND COLOR.

NEST – BIRD

NICO IS AWARE OF OTHER WONDERFUL THINGS HAPPENING AROUND HIM, TOO.

HE CAN FEEL A STRONG WIND BLOWING THROUGH TOWN. THIS WIND IS ALWAYS FULL OF DREAMS.

THIS WIND MAGICALLY MOVES THE CLOUDS TO FORM DIFFERENT SHAPES.

6 CIRCLE AN ICE CREAM AND A BALL IN THE SKY.

NICO DREAMS OF CLOUDS SHAPING INTO WHATEVER FORM HE WANTS.

IF NICO DREAMS OF A DOG, HE CLOSES HIS EYES TIGHTLY AND WHEN HE OPENS THEM, A DOG APPEARS UP IN THE SKY.

HOWEVER, NICO KNOWS THAT IN REAL LIFE HE CAN'T ALWAYS HAVE WHAT HE WANTS SO MAGICALLY.

HE KNOWS THAT NOTHING IS IMPOSSIBLE. IF HE CAN IMAGINE IT, DREAM ABOUT IT, HE CAN MAKE IT HAPPEN.

7 DRAW A DREAM.

WHEN NICO GROWS A LITTLE OLDER,
HE DISCOVERS THAT HE NEEDS MONEY TO MAKE SOME DREAMS COME TRUE.

NICO IS VERY SMART, HE FIGURES OUT THAT MONEY CAN'T BUY HIM A CLOUD IN THE SKY, OR A SUNSET, OR EVEN HAPPINESS ON A RAINY DAY.

☐ YES ☐ NO

8 OBSERVE THE PICTURES AND CHECK **YES** OR **NO**.

A DREAM I DON'T NEED MONEY TO MAKE IT COME TRUE.

A DREAM I NEED MONEY TO MAKE IT COME TRUE.

☐ YES ☐ NO

☐ YES ☐ NO

☐ YES ☐ NO

☐ YES ☐ NO

☐ YES ☐ NO

SOON, HE REALIZES HE NEEDS MONEY TO BUY THINGS LIKE AN ICE CREAM CONE, A SOCCER BALL, OR A SKATEBOARD.

NICO UNDERSTANDS THAT SOME DREAMS NEED MONEY, OTHERS DON'T, BUT EVERY MATERIAL DREAM HAS A PRICE.

9 LOOK AT THE PICTURES AND CHOOSE **YES** OR **NO**.

	YES	NO
A		
B		
C		
D		
E		
F		

NICO UNDERSTANDS THAT THE PRICE OF THINGS DEPENDS ON HOW DIFFICULT IT IS TO CREATE THEM.

IN HIS MIND, IT IS EASIER TO MAKE AN ICE CREAM CONE THAN TO MAKE A TOY AIRPLANE. THEREFORE, HE NEEDS MORE MONEY TO BUY A TOY AIRPLANE THAN AN ICE CREAM CONE!

10 CIRCLE. WHAT COSTS MORE?

FOR A MOMENT, NICO FEELS SAD, BECAUSE HE KNOWS THAT IF A PERSON HAS NO MONEY, HE CAN'T MAKE DREAMS COME TRUE.

NICO HAS A BRILLIANT IDEA AS HE THINKS OF OTHER DREAMS.

11 COLOR THE ITEMS THAT COST MORE MONEY.

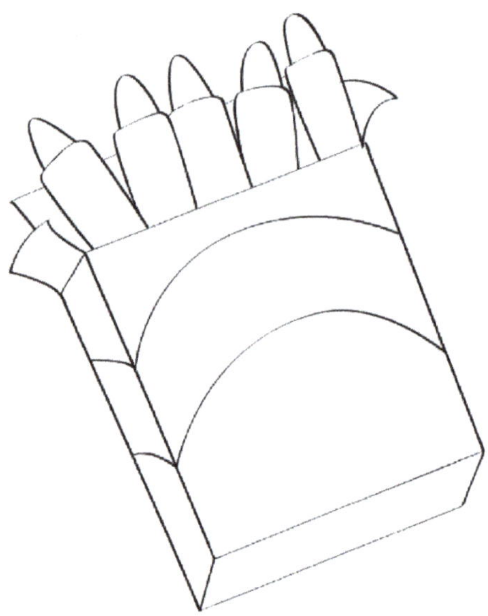

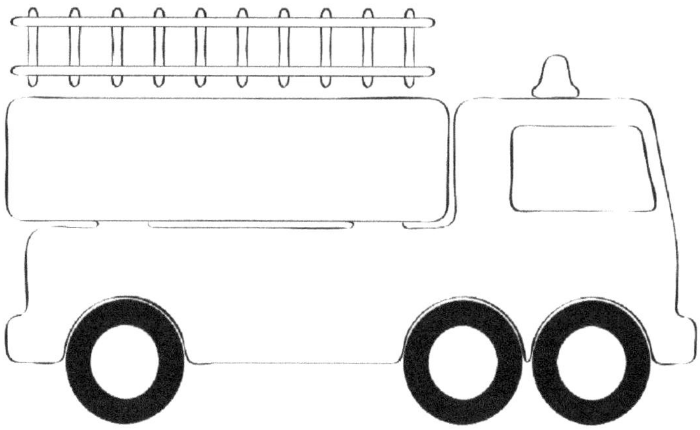

ALL OF A SUDDEN, HE REMEMBERS THE ANT STRUGGLING TO CARRY LEAVES INTO THE ANTHILL AND THE BIRD BUILDING ITS NEST ONE TWIG AT A TIME.

NICO THINKS MONEY IS LIKE THAT. IT IS SOMETHING YOU GET A LITTLE BIT AT A TIME TO BUILD DREAMS.

ANYONE CAN DO IT: THOSE WHO HAVE MUCH OR LITTLE MONEY, OR THOSE WHO ARE BIG OR SMALL.

12 CIRCLE NICO SAVING FOR HIS DREAM.

NICO IS VERY SMART. HE KNOWS A LOT OF THINGS NOW!

THIS IS THE STORY OF A BOY WHO FINDS A WAY TO MAKE DREAMS COME TRUE BY SAVING A SINGLE PENNY AT A TIME.

HE GOES OUT INTO THE WORLD TEACHING HIS METHODOLOGY TO PEOPLE HE MEETS ALONG THE WAY.

13 DRAW THE DREAMS YOU WANT TO COME TRUE.

A VERY SPECIAL MESSAGE FROM DSOP

To the teachers or parents/guardians

Congratulations, you just took the first step towards an investment with an invaluable return: prosperity, in every moment of your family's life, beginning with your young student!

The DSOP Methodology illustrates how important it is to have dreams in our lives, and above all how to achieve them. It focuses upon behavioural development, with the goal of creating a healthier financial life. This makes it possible to build a life filled with accomplishments.

The DSOP books, courses and educational programmes for children and young people also include content which extends to family members and school staff. The guidance given, both in the manuals and projects offered to teachers and from the DSOP advisors and pedagogical support team, will help your young student to transform their life, inspired by the captivating and entrepreneurial paths taken by the characters in the stories.

There is growing awareness internationally of the importance of incorporating Financial Education in school curriculums. In some cases, this is combined with teaching students to develop conscious behaviour around consumption practices. The UN proposed the 17 Sustainable Development Goals (SNGs) and included Responsible

MENSAGEM MUITO ESPECIAL DA DSOP

Aos responsáveis pelos alunos ou seus familiares

Parabéns, você acaba de dar o primeiro passo rumo a um investimento de retorno inestimável: a prosperidade em todos os momentos da vida da sua família, começando pelo jovem estudante da sua casa!

A Metodologia DSOP mostra a importância dos sonhos em nossas vidas e, especialmente, como alcançá-los. O foco está no desenvolvimento comportamental para uma vida financeira mais saudável. Assim, é possível construir uma vida cheia de realizações.

Os livros, cursos e programas educacionais para crianças e jovens também são complementados por conteúdos que se estendem à sua família e funcionários da escola. Com o apoio das orientações dos manuais e projetos oferecidos aos professores e da assessoria e suporte pedagógicos da DSOP, eles ajudarão o jovem estudante a transformar a vida inspirado nas adoráveis trajetórias empreendedoras das personagens.

A BNCC (Base Nacional Comum Curricular) tornou obrigatório nas escolas públicas e privadas o ensino de Educação Financeira nos Anos Iniciais e Finais do Ensino Fundamental, porém voltado para que os alunos desenvolvam um comportamento de consumo consciente.
A própria ONU propõe os 17 Objetivos de Sustentabilidade

MENSAJE MUY ESPECIAL DE DSOP

A las familias de los alumnos o sus responsables

¡Felicitaciones! Usted acaba de dar el primer paso rumbo a una inversión de valor inestimable: la prosperidad en todos los momentos de la vida de su familia, empezando por los jóvenes estudiantes de su casa.

La Metodología DSOP potencia la valoración de los sueños en nuestras vidas y, especialmente, cómo alcanzarlos. El énfasis está en el desarrollo comportamental hacia una vida financiera más saludable, pues así es posible construir una vida de realizaciones. Los libros, cursos y programas educacionales para jóvenes son también complementados por contenidos que alcanzan a sus familias y toda la comunidad escolar.

Con el apoyo de las orientaciones de los manuales, proyectos, asesoría y soporte pedagógicos de la Editorial DSOP, los profesores ayudarán a su joven estudiante a transformar su vida, inspirado en las adorables trayectorias emprendedoras de los personajes.

En Brasil hay leyes que han vuelto obligatoria en las escuelas públicas y privadas la enseñanza de la Educación Financiera volcada hacia el desarrollo de un comportamiento de consumo consciente. La misma ONU propone 17 Objetivos de Sustentabilidad para la Humanidad e incluye Consumption, refiriéndose exactamente a esa cuestión.

Consumption, referring to precisely this objective.

For over 10 years, Reinaldo Domingos PhD has been sharing his methodology with the world via the DSOP group. It has brought great success not only for him, but also for all the Financial Educators and Financial Therapists who have graduated during this decade, as well as, more recently, through franchises. Its efficiency has been proven not only in practice, but also by the academic and scientific world; his methodology has been championed in the United States at universally commended master, doctoral and post-doctoral levels.

When it comes to behaviour, the best way to develop it swiftly and achieve efficient results is to start as early as possible and maintain consistency. We need to begin preparing ourselves for adult life in childhood, and by doing so we can achieve financial independence earlier than previous generations, and dedicate our efforts and time towards realising our own dreams and those of the people we love.

So, how does this transformational methodology work? Learn more and win a free e-book on DSOP Financial Education Methodology, visit the link or QR Code on the back cover of this book.

para a Humanidade e incluiu o Consumption, referindo-se exatamente a esse objetivo.

Há mais de 10 anos, por meio do Grupo DSOP, o PhD Reinaldo Domingos tem compartilhado com o mundo sua metodologia vivenciada com sucesso não só por ele, como também por todos os Educadores Financeiros e Terapeutas Financeiros formados ao longo dessa década, além do trabalho mais recente com os franqueados. Não só a prática comprovou sua eficiência, mas também o mundo acadêmico e científico, pois sua metodologia também foi defendida nos Estados Unidos em níveis de mestrado, doutorado e pós-doutorado aprovados com louvor e de forma unânime.

Quando falamos de comportamento, a melhor maneira de desenvolvê-lo rapidamente rumo aos resultados eficientes, é começando o quanto antes e mantendo a continuidade. Desde criança, temos que nos preparar para a vida adulta; assim, poderemos nos tornar independentes mais cedo que as gerações anteriores e direcionar nossos esforços e tempo, a partir de então, para a realização de sonhos próprios e os de quem amamos.

Mas, como é essa metodologia transformadora? Saiba mais e ganhe um e-book sobre a Metodologia DSOP de Educação Financeira, por meio do QR Code atrás deste livro.

Hace más de 10 años, por medio del Grupo DSOP, el PhD Reinaldo Domingos ha compartido su metodología vivenciada con éxito no solo por él sino por todos los Educadores Financieros y Terapeutas financieros formados en sus cursos. Además de toda la comprobación práctica, está también el reconocimiento académico y científico, pues la Metodología DSOP ha sido defendida en los EEUU en niveles de máster, de doctorado y posdoctorado.

Cuando se trata de comportamiento, para garantizar resultados eficientes en el futuro, lo mejor es desarrollarlo lo más pronto posible, además de mantener su continuidad. Desde niños, debemos ir preparándonos para los principales retos de la vida adulta, para volvernos independientes financieramente aún antes de la edad en la que las generaciones anteriores lo lograban. Así, podremos concentrarnos a partir de entonces no solo en disfrutar de los sueños ya alcanzados, sino también a multiplicarlos e incluir a quienes amamos en esa trayectoria.

Pero, ¿cómo es esa metodología transformadora? Para saberlo, infórmese mejor y adquiera su e-book sobre Educación Financiera en el código QR detrás de este libro.

REINALDO DOMINGOS WAS BORN IN CASA BRANCA, A SMALL TOWN IN THE STATE OF SÃO PAULO, BRAZIL. HIS FATHER WAS A RAILWAY WORKER AND HIS MOTHER A SELF-EMPLOYED WORKER. AT THE AGE OF 12, HE DREAMED OF HAVING A BIKE. HE CREATED A METHOD OF SAVING SOME MONEY EVERY MONTH TO MAKE HIS DREAM COME TRUE. THIS METHOD BECAME THE BASIS OF THE DSOP METHODOLOGY: A SIMPLE AND EFFICIENT WAY OF MANAGING MONEY, CHANGING CONSUMPTION HABITS AND MAKING DREAMS COME TRUE.